AMUSING THE ANGELS

Poems by
Stewart Florsheim

BLUE LIGHT PRESS ✦ 1ST WORLD PUBLISHING

1ST WORLD
PUBLISHING

SAN FRANCISCO ✦ FAIRFIELD ✦ DELHI

Winner, 2022 Blue Light Book Award

Amusing the Angels

Copyright ©2023, Stewart Florsheim

BLUE LIGHT PRESS
www.bluelightpress.com
bluelightpress@aol.com

1ST WORLD PUBLISHING
PO Box 2211
Fairfield, IA 52556
www.1stworldpublishing.com

BOOK & COVER DESIGN
Melanie Gendron
melaniegendron999@gmail.com

COVER ART
Creation/ Schepping by Chagall, Marc (1887-1985) - Jewish Historical Museum, Netherlands - Public Domain.
https://www.europeana.eu/item/270/resource_document_jhm_museum_M009247

FIRST EDITION

Library of Congress Cataloging-in-Publication Data

ISBN: 978-1-4218-3528-0

Praise for *Amusing the Angels*

In this richly diverse mélange of human lives, many actual and many imagined, Stewart Florsheim embraces the light and the dark much as his beloved Rembrandt employed chiaroscuro to reveal the complexity of a single individual, and thus, all individuals. Florsheim's vision is encompassing, with room enough for the emotional convolutions of family, Holocaust survivors, spiritual seekers, intimate partners, world travelers, artists, and even total strangers. Taking his cue from Aristotle, and perhaps from the painters he admires, he approaches life from the particular. Pulsing through the array of details is the tempered passion of someone who considers desire as "the trembling to be whole."

— Thomas Centolella, author of *Almost Human*

Here, as in his previous collections, Stewart Florsheim combines closely observed detail with moments of transcendence—sometimes metaphorical, other times supernatural—that conjure the lost world of European Jewry, the intimate sphere of his family life, and the lines of blood and spirit that connect the two. He steps into famous paintings as if through a looking glass and renders public events with evocative brushwork. Having read his poetry for more than thirty years, I am impressed by how consistent his body of work is and grateful for the rich worldview it provides.

— Scott Norton, author of *Developmental Editing: A Guide for Freelancers, Authors, and Publishers, Second Edition* (forthcoming 2023)

In his third full-length poetry collection from Blue Light Press, Stewart Florsheim wrestles with the possibilities and contradictions of what it means today to be a man. The child of a Holocaust survivor, he lends his poetic voice to the lost and dispossessed, "amusing the angels," perhaps, by evoking his forebears, with insight and tenderness, in all their flawed humanity. Many of these poems can be read as prayers, as when he recalls his adolescent terror at facing the high jump in gym class, "hoping my wings won't get mangled/as I ascend above the trees/into the incandescent light." Without ignoring any of the familiar impulses or vanities of a husband, father, and successful man of the world, he nonetheless embraces the vulnerability of his anima. Making pesto with his daughter, he confides how much he loves the smell of basil, evoking Italian landscapes he hopes to share with her someday. His ekphrastic poems could be a volume all of their own, filled with the color, light, and stories of the paintings that come under his knowledgeable and imaginative gaze. Everything in daily life, from taking out the trash to sexual desire –"the trembling to be whole" – comes under the poet's lens as he strives to "discover the pleasures of being vigilant."

– Barbara Quick, author of *The Light on Sifnos* and *What Disappears*

Amusing the Angels is a Tree of Life in the garden of poetry. The roots of this tree grow deep into Jewish ancestry, deep into an American childhood haunted by Hitler. Its trunk grows strong in word and in image. Its branches reach out into many worlds – dreams, desire, daughters, a mother who is "always alive and dead," far-flung travels, paintings that tell love stories. Its highest branches reach up into the heavens, where "God speaks to Abraham" and "the angels are amused," one imagines, to see how the poet can turn horror and sorrow into prayer, and into visionary poetry that celebrates life. Stewart Florsheim has written us a blessing of a book for our own troubled times.

– Naomi Ruth Lowinsky, author of *The Faust Woman Poems* and
Death and His Lorca

What stays with us, what passes into the realm of nightmare and fantasy and metaphor, as we move individually through our lives, carrying with us the inherited experiences of those who came before us? Harkening back to the Holocaust and following traces of his family's experiences through his own days growing up in post-war Washington Heights and into his adulthood on the West Coast, Stewart Florsheim offers up an arresting collection of poems – poignant, intimate, ironic, attentive, and certainly heartfelt – exploring what it means to endure, to thrive, as a modern American with a heritage in the German refugee/immigrant experience as a template. These are poems that will touch your heart as the poet bears witness to what it takes to come to terms with the ordinary human challenges of 20th and 21st century America, what it takes to write the simple lines that reveal the complex stoicism, flights of the imagination, and stubborn grace that helped countless individuals and families on their decades-long intergenerational journey from the horrors of the Holocaust to the ambiguities of the American promised land.

Stewart Florsheim's new book, *Amusing the Angels*, is an intimate invitation to readers to enter into the poetic memoir of a man fully immersed in family life. He provides a rich panorama of what it can be, to be a fully engaged father, son, husband, and historian, not only of family life but of spiritual and political life. This is a book full of vigor, tenderness, and acknowledgment. Even Socrates would agree, an examined life, worth living, worth reading about.

In *Amusing the Angels*, Stewart Florsheim shows his surprising range in exploring grief and sexuality. The past and the present are hauntingly braided together throughout the collection. From his reflections on art and personal histories of close family members in older generations surviving the Holocaust, to his mother's depression and death, to raising his own family, this collection conveys a sense of loss – what could have been – mixed with desire.

Acknowledgments

"Jerusalem," "Diaspora," and "Tel Aviv Promenade" first appeared in *J The Jewish News of Northern California*, November 1, 2012

"Message: Sitka Sound" first appeared in *Canary*, Issue 57, Summer 2022

"The Journey Back" first appeared in *Minyan*, Issue 4, Summer 2022

"Today" and "The Invisible" first appeared in *Pandemic Puzzle Poems*, Blue Light Press, 2021

Special thanks to the following individuals for their feedback and support: Tom Centolella, Diane Frank, Ellen Holz, Scott Norton, Judy Rosloff, and the members of the poetry workshop hosted by Gail and Charles Entrekin.

Table of Contents

2.

3.

A Breezy Time of Day

after the painting, *Adam and Eve Expelled from Paradise*, by Marc Chagall, 1961

The angel seems bemused
as she expels Adam and Eve from the garden.
After all, they don't seem displeased:
They see each other for the first time
and will soon abandon their embarrassment
for joy and, in time, for pain.

Their curiosity is ravenous.
The musky scent of the earth
will invigorate them
and arouse their hunger.
They will have children
and learn how to nourish them.

Their knowledge will be a light,
often disclosing the inadequacy
of the words they use
to express their wonder,
their anguish,
and their resolve.

They will find that time is the enemy
and can cancel out even
their greatest accomplishments.

They will observe animals that send signals,
often to other species,
to alert them about nearby predators.

They will watch ravens mourn
when members of their conspiracies
die or get killed.

They will grieve for their son
after he's killed at the hands of his brother.
They will bury him and weep.

They will have another child.

They will never turn back.

1

I could hear the clock ticking,
presumably alluding to the passage of time
while in fact annulling it.

– Louise Glück, from "The Denial of Death"

Narrating the Stones

Stolpersteine installation, Frankfurt, May, 2022

At the end of the ceremony,
the young schoolchildren
peel away from the crowd.
It looks like a movie
that begins in real time
but then I imagine
the time slows,
almost to a standstill:
The children are in school.
They're learning about Hitler
and the camps.
They see pictures
and ask questions.
Kinder auch?[1]

The teacher tells them
about a Jewish family
who lived a few blocks away,
at Zeil 51 –
a father, mother, two children.
Kristallnacht.
Dachau.
New York.
Stolpersteine.

Back in real time,
the children rush
to the stones
to drop roses
on the names

---

[1] Children too?

1

of my grandfather,
grandmother,
mother,
uncle.

One of them
struggles
to look up at me,
puzzled
by the weight
of remorse.

Jewish Quarter, Nasielsk, Poland, 1938

Footage from a street scene:
Men wearing their black coats and skull caps,
women shopping at *Spozywczy* grocery,
people eating at a kosher restaurant,
families exiting the synagogue.

Shmuel Tyk and Faiga Milchberg at 01:11:25,
Chaim Talmud and Shmuel Tyk at 01:11:56,
Simcha Rotstein and Avrum Kubel at 01:12:04,
Yitzhak Borts at 01:12:09,
Srebro at 01:12:11,
Chaim Nusen Cwajghaft at 01:12:24,
Chezkiah and Chaim Nusen Cwajghaft at 01:12:34.

A few of the boys run in front
of the man shooting the film,
vying for the camera's attention,
amused that someone
wants to record their lives.

The Journey Back

Inspired by journal entries made by my great uncle, Adolph Hess,
June 1939, en route from Cuba back to Europe on the S.S. St. Louis

Dr. Loewe was the smart one: he cut his wrists
and jumped into the ocean before we left Cuba.
His trail of blood looked like a whirlpool
sucking him into another world –
but then a well-meaning passenger
surprised all of us and jumped in to save him.

> They're trying to make us feel better by offering choices
> at the other end: Antwerp, Amsterdam, Boulogne Sur Mer.
> But some of us have already been to the camps
> and believe there will only be one destination
> with multiple names – each of them a curse:
> Dachau, Buchenwald, Sachsenhausen.

The children don't stop crying and we hope
their screams will somehow reach God. (Yes,
some of us are still believers, now more than ever!)
He will see our boat going back and forth
and if we're all destined for hell, we pray the St. Louis
will sink before we reach the mainland.

> Our Vera and Ilse are sick.
> For all the dancing they did on the way to Cuba,
> it seems like their feet are suddenly made of lead.
> They ask us what will happen when we get back
> and Yette and I keep saying, *We'll see,*
> but I fear they detect the quiver in my voice.

Oh, how we dreamed about the tall sugar cane –
candy that grows right out of the earth.
I imagined sitting on a veranda wearing a Panama hat,

smoking those fine fat Cabañas cigars.
Ilse learned Spanish (even a few words about love).
Vera practiced salsa with a pretend boyfriend.

But the Cubans wouldn't let us in.

The Americans wouldn't let us in.

We sailed past Florida and I remembered
hearing about the big, fancy hotels,
the warm, crystal-clear water and now all I can see
are the machine guns pointing at us,
policemen yelling and, closer to shore –

yachts, the people basking in the sun.

The Great Aunts

I'm six years old – and on the street I'm scared of them, especially Aunt Marion with her thin white hair, stout body, sauerkraut breath. When I see her in the candy store, she shuffles towards me and plants a wet kiss on the corner of my lip.

Inside, they're curiosities. They sit at the kitchen table playing gin rummy, smell of instant coffee and cherry-cheese Danish spilling from the room. The table is oval, made from Formica that looks like white marble, veins as visible as those on Aunt Martha's hands. They seem to form an "M" and I wonder if that's the way she received her name. Aunt Henrietta, my parents used to whisper, converted to Christian Science. I imagine her pouring liquid from one test tube to another, a Christ-like ghost eventually filling the room.

I can't tell the difference between German and English, other than when they speak German, there's a hush: the nanny who felt entitled to take the Persian lamb coat, the lout from the SS who beat up my mother, my uncle who was fed castor oil in Auschwitz and then forced to sit in his waste.

I stand in the doorway, fingers screwed into my ears. I may be scraping out words or digging for something else – a source before there was language, the whooshing of liquid that muffles every sound.

Woman Gardening in Ft. Tryon Park, New York City

She might be in the backyard of her home near Munich:
May, 1938, 12 years old, moving the geraniums
from one part of the garden to another. Her family
has just finished Sunday lunch – boiled beef
(instead of the usual *Sauerbraten*), fried potatoes,
a green salad – and even before dessert they ask her,
Möchtest du zum Spielen in den Garten gehen?[2]
She thinks the question odd, of course she wouldn't,
she couldn't wait to see the surprise they might have found –
oranges, the first strawberries, a small piece of chocolate.

The woman digs up the geraniums, straightens her back,
then looks around to find a spot that might offer some shade.
For moments, she even gazes beyond the Hudson,
raising her hands to shield her eyes from the morning sun.

---

[2] Would you like to go play in the garden?

Origins

Grandmother and her sisters whisper around the kitchen table.
My parents warn me there are two kinds of German: *Hör mal!*[3]

Father at *Yizkor*,[4] fasting, a bottle of smelling salts in his pocket.
In the *Kaddish*,[5] the majesty of heaven and earth.

When I'm a boy, Mother, crying, locks herself in the bathroom.
My girlfriend refuses to go to her studio – seventh day in a row.

Sister laughs at my high voice, calls me *mama's boy*.
Words flutter inside my mouth: so many letters.

In second grade, I chase Arlene Rosenblatt around her dining
      room table.
When you and I make love, you promise to give me everything.

[3.] Listen up!
[4.] Memorial prayer (literally, "remember")
[5.] Mourner's prayer (literally, "sanctification")

Eleanor Roosevelt Visits the Hood

When Eleanor Roosevelt comes to Washington Heights, Father wants me to go with him to hear her speak. I'm almost ten years old, and even though Father and I don't do much together, he insists. He even puts on a clean shirt and his suede jacket before we leave our tiny apartment, and walk up the hill to Bennett Park.

Roosevelt is speaking from the back of a pick-up truck. The audience is mostly German Jews and Puerto Ricans. There's often tension between us, but everyone claps when she talks about the importance of equal job opportunities. She mentions how excited she is that John Kennedy is now our president because he's against the separation of Blacks and whites. She discusses the importance of books, which makes me happy because I spend most of my time reading.

Father is beaming. He's a butcher, without much time or interest in politics. He's probably less taken by her words than the thought of Roosevelt being a few blocks from our apartment. His expression doesn't change when she ends with one of her famous lines: *Do one thing every day that scares you.*

When I think about scary things, I think about Mother always yelling at Father – calling him *stupid* in front of my friends and challenging him to take more of an interest in his son. I think about Father not responding to her – except for the few times when he gets so angry, he turns bright red. When that happens, I get sick to my stomach because I know he's about to explode. His tirades against Mother fill the apartment, the walls trembling as he charges from room to room.

Mother always expects my unspoken allegiance but, during these rare episodes, I root for him all the way.

Father and I walk back down the hill stopping, as usual, to greet all the people he knows. I don't think about the other dimension of fear but as I walk beside Father that day, I reach for his hand, as though I always knew it would be there, waiting for mine.

Ritual

Every week, my father lays
his small turquoise towel down
on the gray Formica kitchen table,
opens the gold-plated case,
and takes out his nail file, scissors, clipper.
He starts by cleaning each nail slowly,
the file going from one end of his nail
to the other to clean out
the specs of fat and blood.
I stand and watch, 11 years old,
wondering how hands
that would sooner carry sides of beef
than touch another human being
could require so much attention.

Gym

Junior high school: I stand in line
waiting to jump over the high bar.
Nothing in life has prepared me for this –
not my gym teacher with his back-slapping *attaboys*;
not Father who became a refugee from
intimacy, Mother yelling like a TV character
he finally put on mute;
certainly not Mother who worried
each time I left the apartment.

I know I'll have to jump
and that something may break, but what's
a bone in the face of ridicule –
so I begin to run, imagining I'm a plane,
hoping my wings won't get mangled
as I ascend above the trees
into the incandescent light.

Translucent

An operation
on Father's heart
and I open up mine:
We shuffle
down the hospital corridor,
silently,
arms locked.
I am not sure
who is supporting whom
as we fasten our hold
and move
into winter light.

Appearance

When I'm a boy, my left eye turns inward.
Mother has a revelation: I think too much.

A McDonalds in southern California goes *Feng Shui* and sales double.
At a restaurant in Hong Kong, my wife lifts her legs to let a rat run by.

The government prints more and more money.
Houses collapse: trees grow wild.

A woman on the bus reads an article, *30 Ways to Entice Your Lover*.
At the ballet, three couples do interpretations of Chopin's *Nocturnes*.

Mother says her depression gets so bad she can't see.
In temple, at night, the stained glass is luminous.

Dropping Off My Two-Year-Old at Daycare

She's like a roly-poly
bundled up in her thick blue parka.
She tries to balance herself on the curb
but can't, so one of the five-year-olds
walks over to help her.
I see them holding hands in my rear-view mirror
as I speed off to catch the 7:25 train.
I can almost imagine I may never see her again
so I begin to count her freckles
the way I was doing it for her
while she was eating her oatmeal.
I count them all the way to the station
and then on the train from San Francisco to Mt. View.
I keep fighting the urge I have to fall asleep.

Making Pesto with My Daughter

My six-year-old considers each basil leaf before pulling it,
every so often asking, *Daddy, is this one OK?*
We chat about school, her girlfriends, movies,
how she thinks Pocahontas is a good role model
because she saves people. I ask her
if she would like to save people one day
and she giggles, *Maybe.* So much depends
on this preparation – the way we assemble
the basil, garlic, pine nuts, olive oil;
our talk about the things that matter:
her best friend threatening to abandon her
if she doesn't give up her other friends,
her fear of playing soccer on the local team,
the boys she likes but can't invite over
because it's not cool to be friendly with them.

I tell her how much I love the smell of basil,
how it reminds me of the open-air markets in Lucca
and yes, we need to go to Italy together.
Islands with names like Lipari, Stromboli, their beaches
so white they gleam under the stars.
The ice-cream that tastes like pure hazelnuts.
Sculptures like Michelangelo's *Captives*, so real
they seem to be breaking free from the stone.
The abundance of figs the size of her small fist.

My Eight-Year-Old Is Learning Cursive

In her dreams, she draws neon *O's*
across the sky; they're so large
they light up the city, the loops
offer a space to practice cartwheels.
She was excited when she learned block letters
but nothing like this, the words themselves
becoming art forms, some so full of life
they become what they represent –
a dog, a tulip, a butterfly.
I watch her at her desk, her thoughts
trying to keep up with the strokes –
there, the final loop of the *B*,
the curve of another *S*,
but already she's inside her story:
The garden is beginning to blossom,
her girlfriends are arriving with their gifts,
the party has just begun.

Lessons

We're walking through the back woods of Lake Tahoe –
Orli holding one of my hands, Maya the other –
imagining the woods are full of elves,
some of them so tiny they ride the backs of banana slugs.
And then we see the bear ambling alongside us
no more than 20 feet away, not sure if he's part of our story,
the Woody Allen character that appears just as you imagine him.
I forget what I'm supposed to do so I break into
The Wheels on the Bus Go Round and Round and try to flail my arms,
but I only have one at my disposal, Orli clutching the other one
so tightly I see traces of her nails on my hand for years.
Maya has broken free and starts to chase him,
the big stuffed bear on her bed suddenly come to life.
I start to run towards her yelling *Stop*, but Orli is frozen now,
her small body trying to keep me in place. Lucky for us,
the bear is preoccupied and ambles away, and I'm left
with the remnants of our story: When elves reach a certain age
they learn to become afraid of scary things, and that's good –
although I'm as baffled as Maya, who is about to burst into tears.

Taking Out the Trash

When it comes to housework, the only task I can perform with a certain amount of competence and satisfaction is that of taking out the rubbish. – Italo Calvino, *La poubelle agréée*

I walk from room to room emptying
the smaller bins into a larger one, my tendency
after years of studying Aristotle
to approach life from the particular.
And who we are begins to materialize
from the refuse of our week:
lines from a poem based on a painting by Manet,
the scent from a condom wrapper,
broken doll, torn-up math homework,
empty Merlot bottles and pints of mango sorbet.
Early the next morning, Waste Management
will come noisily as if to alert us –
they're about to mix our trash with the neighbors',
people we know but hardly well enough
to share this amount of intimacy.

Learning to Dance

On Mother's last trip to California,
she can barely walk up the ramp from the plane.
She holds one of the railings with both hands,
looks towards me and smiles,
See, I can do it, her legs buckling,
her body slowly making its ascent.

Mother starts off using a shopping cart,
then she calls the walker her boyfriend.
When the wheelchair arrives, we have our game:
I lift her up and we pretend to dance –
sometimes a waltz, others a foxtrot.
The room begins to spin and we never stop falling.

Mother's Phone Book

I still have it after all these years –
a small binder with tabs for each letter of the alphabet.
It reads like a personal history
including all my parents' aunts and uncles,
first and second cousins in the US and Israel,
nieces, nephews, neighbors,
doctors, a few of her favorite hairdressers,
the ladies who play canasta and gin rummy,
the people who play Scrabble with her
carefully listed under 'S'.
It's Mother's early version of Facebook,
with names crossed out if the people died,
cheated when they played cards,
or didn't offer her rides to the swim club.

At the front of the binder, on the first tab,
she wrote down the names of all the contacts
at her hospice. Her hand was shaky,
she was scared she might suffocate,
the ALS quickly immobilizing her body:
Jacob Perlow Hospice, with phone numbers
for Jill, Lynn, Wesley, Maura –
her nurses, doctor, social worker. At the end,
she wouldn't have been able to dial a number
or talk to anyone, each word weighed down
by its letters. She would have reached for her
phone book and it would have fallen to the floor,
the rings opening, the pages
flying around the room like silent crows.

Source

When I find Mother in her room alone –
eyes half opened,
locked on the heavens,
mouth in the shape of an *O* –
I imagine falling into it,
until my breath is nesting
inside her non-breath:
the first sound.

     • • •

In a dream, I try to describe to Father
my trek through the Himalayas.
A movie screen appears and we step into it,
the air so thin we cannot speak.
I want to tell him he's no longer alive
but it doesn't seem to matter.
We're climbing a mountain and he's walking ahead.
Every so often he turns to make sure I'm still there.

     • • •

When I'm a boy, Mother takes me along to shop
for her clothing. She tries on dress after
dress, asking me which style is most becoming.
She says she still has her waist, but the best part
about her body has always been her legs.
She pulls up her dress to show me, and then says
Father doesn't really care how she looks or dresses.
Ist doch alles gut!,[6] he says, under his breath.

     • • •

[6.] It's all good!

On my parents' first date, Mother is shy.
They go to the Tea Room in Washington Heights
and talk about life after Hitler – the meat market, two children.
That's all they need for now. Later, Mother will read books,
talk to her American neighbors, meet other parents.
Father will come home with parts of animals
set in aspic – tongues, kidneys, hearts.
Mother will begin to cry for no apparent reason.

The Day After Mother Dies

I walk the long walk down 181st St
to remove the securities from her safe deposit box.
It's the same walk I did when we went to temple on Saturdays,
Grandmother on one side of me, Father on the other,

the sanctuary filled with Germans, survivors like my grandfather
of Auschwitz or Dachau, the request on one of his
postcards home so simple it still haunts me:
Bitte schick mir Butter, um meine Nerven zu beruhigen.[7]

Every week, I had no clue how the *shul* could remain faithful.
The banker asks me to put my key into the tiny metal door
while he puts in his master key and, in perfect time,
we turn, as in a well-rehearsed dance, then

the banker slides out the long box and walks me
into a private booth. At the top of the box,
a yellow post-it note from Mother with the word *Enjoy.*
Her sense of humor, to be sure, and I smile

as I rifle through the securities I already know about,
stocks from General Motors and Con Ed but,
at the bottom, a large envelope that simply says
Germany. I turn it over and shake it out – the yellow star,

passports, visa, boat ticket – artifacts I always asked for
but Mother would say *Enough already, the Holocaust
affected you more than it affected me*, and I would
roll my eyes and ask more questions about how she knew

[7.] Please send me butter to ease my nerves.

her father was arriving home from Dachau at 2 a.m. one morning
and she bolted out of bed and ran down to the train station
to meet him. I turned every story around in my head,
turning corners with more questions until I could visualize

my uncle in a jail cell being fed castor oil, the stench, the
          barking dogs;
his silence when I touched the numbers branded on his arm.
Perhaps that's what Mother meant by the post-it note,
          the simple word
to underlie the irony that helped us both endure: *Enjoy*.

Triptych

Picking up the receiver, I struggle
to keep it at a distance – wailing sounds –
not my 18-year-old, hysterical, 3000 miles away.

I come up with a ruse – *a business trip to New York* –
and meet my daughter at the alumni house.
Inside, students walk by, arms hooked together,
laughing about a date with someone
who turned out to be a real jerk,
or chatting about a recent trip to the Met
to complete a paper on Rembrandt.
In the main salon, a triptych by Violet Oakley –
the center dominated by a young woman
in the heavens, holding up her child:
a woman clothed with the sun,
and the moon at her feet,
and upon her head a crown of twelve stars.[8]

My daughter wants to know
what's wrong with her.
I remind her of the times when she was a girl
and called us at 1 a.m. to pick her up from sleepovers –
the way she looked walking down the front stairs
in her flannel nightgown, crying,
her brown bear clutched under one arm,
her yellow blanket under the other.
We laugh, forgetting that there may not be words
to explain those nights either,
the quizzical looks of the parents,
their smiles unnavigable.

---

[8] *Revelation 12:1*

Hunger

Walking through the locked hallways,
I imagine maniacal sounds – people howling,
the indecipherable wails of a man
tearing apart a book as he looks for
the one sentence that will save him.
Instead, there is only the blaring
silence marked by squeaking soles.

In the corridor for people who will not eat,
there are no mirrors, only Hockney posters –
blue sky, blue pool, green palms, sun.
The hall appears too cheerful
for the young girls who seem to float by,
girls who may want to be invisible
or defined by the spaces they have emptied.

My daughter does not want to eat. I think
I can understand: there's purity in restraint.
The body becomes a temple of denial
and grace. She waves to us from her room
and I recall the days when she stopped eating,
my wife and I finally raging at each other –
the hunger beginning to consume our lives.

November

An alarming email
from my daughter's roommates
and then the long drive down to L.A.
filled with thoughts
about things we should have
done differently,
things we knew but pretended
that we didn't because,
like everything else,
knowledge has its time.
Highway I-5 goes on forever,
without forgiveness.
We have sun,
howling winds,
gusts of rain.
Did someone say
California doesn't have weather?
The fronds on the palm trees rage.

Precipice

1.

In my dream, I wander through the old apartment building.
I know all my neighbors are dead but when I ring their bells
and say my name, they open their doors without hesitation.
It takes them some time to undo their multiple locks –
the police bars, deadbolts, door chains. I wonder
if they've been locked up like this for years,
most of them refugees from Hitler's Germany, consumed
by the fears they secure on their side of the doors.

2.

The old ladies pinch my cheeks even though
I'm as old as they were when I lived in the building.
They speak to me in German and invite me in,
offer me layer cake and *Manner Schnitten* from Austria.
Die Tage sind lang, they say, *aber die Zeit geht schnell vorbei*[9].
They all know my parents have been ill and ask me
how they're doing. I tell them they've been dying
for years, but they refuse to let go.

3.

The elevator ends on the sixth floor.
To get to the roof, I need to climb a flight of steep stairs
and push open the heavy metal door. To the south,
the George Washington Bridge is lined with traffic.
To the west, I can see the Golden Gate. The sun
is rising and I hear a multitude of voices:
my children, wife, friends. I can't decipher their words
but the sounds are dissonant and sweet.

[9.] The days are long but the time goes fast.

2

God's truth, each thing carries its opposite
within… God's truth, that's how things go,
that's how the world is: each thing is double.

– David Diop, from *At Night All Blood is Black*
(as translated by Anna Moschovakis)

Ascent

I try to surface from sleep but dreams are my quicksand.
You hook your arm into mine, no questions asked.

A beached whale becomes a horse that gallops into the ocean.
We crash into each other, wave upon wave.

Eating with my father-in-law, my meal starts to resemble him.
Father never stood a chance.

I climb the circular staircase of the old apartment building.
My children's idea of fun: going down the up escalator.

Mother always alive and dead.
The heavens have never been this transparent.

Prophesies

Mother confides in me about how awful
Father is. He doesn't understand her the way I do.
I'll grow up to be the perfect son and husband.
When I'm about to get married, she tells my fiancée
that I'm a great guy, good-natured and patient,
but she would never want to be married to me.

• • •

A girlfriend meets me in Kabul. She knows
I don't love her, but she persists. On the train through Iran
we have sex, and when she calls out my name,
I focus on the sounds of the train, the hissing
and squeaking, the iron gliding on iron and I imagine
sparks illuminating the hot night.

• • •

A woman my mother's age wants to be lovers.
She comes back night after night with Za'atar
to sprinkle on dark bread, Hungarian poetry, music.
She wants to dance and I don't say no,
the music lifting us outside of time, both of us
now in our twenties, and trembling.

• • •

I meet a woman I think I can love
and want to be with her all the time.
She catches on and tells me, no,
her last lover wouldn't leave her alone.
He was like a bear, pacing around her,
protecting her from the danger she craved.

• • •

In college, my freshmen roommate is gay.
We become friends and then I draw a line.
Months later, I have mono, 104 degrees,
and he brings a man into the room. Delirious,
I imagine a wall-to-wall bed with people
copulating, and then one big sigh lifting the room.

Double Exposure

Was the photo in fact an accident:
the two men apparently gazing into each other,
admiring qualities each one thought he himself lacked –
to be confident walking into a room filled with other men,
or to have the ability to turn one's self-doubt into art.
Or perhaps the men are simply admiring each other:
their openness, sense of humor, irreverence.

Perhaps the photo was not an accident
and the men are proud to show their vulnerability –
after all, how many men would stand in front of a camera
this exposed, all the more so because
they are fully clothed, standing under an elm tree
in a New York City park, early spring,
the trees still bare and regal.

The Prostitute

after the painting, *The Prostitute,* by Amedeo Modigliani, 1918

The woman did not expect this kind of life,
her hand held over her heart to protect her secret:
If her father had not been killed during the war
she would still be minding their millinery shop in Paris,
her father's designs becoming more outlandish
as the threat of war became their reality –
large-brimmed black velvet hats with a wreath of convolvulus,
others made of shirred chestnut satin with a fringe of skunk.
His commentary on war went unnoticed by the
wealthy women who frequented their shop,
the wives of generals and officers,
all of them happy to mask their fear with frivolity.

The woman looks apologetic as she sits on the bed
after she and Amedeo no doubt made love,
her head tilted as though she is about to make a statement:
Amedeo, you silly man, we are both so weak: Take me,
ravage me, but you will never know who I am.

Transits

A hot night for your chilling words to needle my skin.
Rachmaninoff on the car CD, and I'm in an empty ballroom, dancing.

I enter the old apartment building, climb the stairs, and walk down
    the dark corridor.
For the dying, time is endless.

In the *Psalms*, David is worn out, and drenches his bed in tears.
The Kabbalists say God listens when we are most silent.

A man with orange hair invades my dreams.
An astrologer tells me to relax, my Saturn return is almost complete.

Harvey Fite spends 37 years making sculpture out of an abandoned
    quarry.
I write one letter, then the next, and watch words disappear.

On Skye

On the train to the Kyle of Lochalsh,
the woman we sit with is blind
but she knows all of the birds
and the flowers that grow along the tracks:
foxgloves, roses, fuchsia, honeysuckle.

On Skye, we rent a caravan
in a field of heather. It's so small,
when we make love
in the rainy afternoons
we have to collapse everything –
sink, table, chairs –
and the pullout bed fills the space.

After, you rest in the nook of my arm
and we stare out the window
ringing out the names of the birds
as they take flight over the sea:
fulmars, curlews, gulls, egrets.

Pierre Bonnard Walks into the Garden Naked

after the photograph, *Pierre Bonnard Examining the Leaves on a Tree*,
by Marthe Bonnard, 1900-1901

Like the way he steps into his paintings at will –
to make love to Marthe as she lies, sprawled out on their bed,
or to straighten the sheets after the cats ravage them,
searching for the moist odor the lovers leave behind –
Bonnard walks into the garden naked and, seeing a tree
that attracts him, he gathers a few leaves in his hands.

Marthe captures the moment wondering, no doubt, what he's
thinking: perhaps it's about the pattern on the leaves, the veins
like those in her body, long and mysterious, the paths he abhors
and loves, the ones he uses when he follows her to the market,
only to watch her haggle with the butcher about the price of rabbit,
the ones he traces when he kisses her as she steps out of her bath.

The only thing Marthe knows now is the distance between them
is palpable and she wants to run over and loop her arms around him.
A few moments later, he would turn around, look at her
and know her in a way that only Bonnard could, and she would begin
to tremble even before he kisses her, his tongue
always discovering the words that seem to elude her.

Among Men

A friend asks if I want to hunt wild boars with him.
He'd only use a bow and arrow like he did
when he grew up in the backwoods of Wisconsin.
I think about growing up in Manhattan,
the times I was mugged, Father held up at gunpoint.
I laugh and tell him he can't be serious. *Boars are not kosher.*

• • •

In the hot tub, the men talk about the latest football skirmishes,
the star quarterbacks. I haven't a clue but, for once,
I agree that *Someone* could be the best quarterback ever.
I brag about the Australian football game I saw,
all the players who were bloodied and carried off the field
on stretchers, the crowd cheering for each assault.

• • •

A co-worker invites me over for dinner
and when I get to his studio apartment, I see that it's all bed.
He pours me a glass of wine and tells me how good
he'll make me feel, and I won't have to do anything to him.
I tell him no, I just said the same thing to a woman
who was not as kind as I am, and finished her meal before leaving.

• • •

A friend has surgery for prostate cancer
and tells me his time with women may be up.
I want to tell him I've often fantasized about
an absence of desire, how much simpler life might be,
but my words would sound as shallow as my musings –
and what is desire anyway, but the trembling to be whole.

Borders

I feel his voice pulsing on the phone:
the questions, admiration, reports from his
marriage – a land of friendship with little intimacy.
When we walk through a museum,
the stories inside each painting inform our lives:
Corot's *Winter Scene* reminds him of New England,
romping through snow with his children,
but the setting is a cabin in the woods,
a state of mind he never had with his first wife.
Steen's *Merry Company on a Terrace* brings back
my nights carousing in Amsterdam,
but I never stopped being the man in the painting,
partying and gaping at the revelers.

I recall several years back, a psilocybin walk
at Pt. Reyes: I was in the dunes, my friend on the beach
and he ran up to me saying I had a glow,
my body wrapped in a quiet light,
and then he shoved me down, pinned me in place,
his eyes only inches from mine.

Flamenco at the Club Juglar, Madrid

The two dancers sit on the stage,
two musicians behind them.
The guitarist begins and soon after, the singer,
first quietly, and then he starts to wail
about a woman who would not return his love:
Cuando yo me muera, te pío un encargo,
Que con las trenzas de tu pelo negro
me marren las manos.[10]

The dancers close their eyes and then begin to clap
to the beat, dancing with their hands now,
twisting, wringing them. The first one,
the woman in purple, gets up and stares at the singer,
and then she begins just as his song did,
slowly, and then her body twists, stomps, and arches,
then twists, stomps, and arches more quickly,
struggling against the sound of his voice.

The second dancer is quick, determined – the stage
a ribbon of red. She twists from one side of the floor
to the other, her stomping loud enough to drown out
his voice, but then he taunts her with mournful cries.
Her dance becomes quicker, staccato and then she
breaks into a deep arch and rises with a small smile:
the triumph of passion over indifference –
but not a victory for love.

---

[10] When I die, I have a request:
Tie my hands
With the braids of your black hair.

Betrayal

A woman at a bus stop everyday waits for her lover to return.
On a plane over the US, a man tells the attendant it's time for
      him to get off.

When God speaks to Abraham, the angels are amused.
Some say Isaac still lingers on Mt. Moriah.

Noah builds the ark and the world is deluged.
The leaders do not ask for mercy.

Grandfather with his valise packed, ready to go to Dachau.
In New York, my parents cross the street when they hear the
      wrong German.

In a Taoist temple, a man hands a strip of paper to the priest.
A woman receives a note from her lover and weeps.

Clarence Barker and his Dog

after the painting, *Clarence Barker*, by Anders Zorn, 1885

After gazing at a picture of his fiancée,
Clarence looks up and his dog is staring at him,
bewildered. Or perhaps it's Clarence who's bewildered,
wondering how he can possibly love just one woman
for the rest of his life. True, she is stunning,
but what about the other women he fancies,
like Annabel, who plays Liszt so beautifully
he imagines the piano is controlling her –
how else can she play with so much restraint.

In a few moments, he'll mumble something to his dog
about the mysteries of love, and the dog will respond
by licking his face, pleased, as usual, to be his confidant.
And then Clarence will push himself off the divan
and saunter to the piano where he'll play Berlioz,
the *Symphonie Fantastique*, imagining he's walking
in the Jardin du Luxembourg during his honeymoon,
his wife's arm looped tightly inside his.

Hourglass

Walking through Amsterdam's Jordaan, arms locked,
I say to you, *How great it is that we haven't aged,*
forgetting that 30 years have passed,
the Westerkerk visible but silent.

• • •

Petit walks a tightrope between the World Trade Center towers,
the thin air bold, unforgiving.
Around him people tumble without grace,
against their will, and never stop falling.

• • •

The magazine says the baby boomers are at fault:
the debt, wars in Iraq and Afghanistan.
On the car radio, Dylan sings *Knocking on Heaven's Door* –
the bang-bang-bang of his prayer.

• • •

A homeless man walks up Second carrying a fishing rod.
I imagine the sound of a line being thrown across
traffic, a lake stocked with trout, a blue heron
standing in the water pecking at its reflection.

• • •

On the Kloveniersburgwal, a prostitute unpeels
a banana in front of me, smiling. *You want mouth love,* she asks
with a Slavic accent, the words in Dutch
growling as they trail me down a cobblestone street.

In a Dream

I come face-to-face
with a tiger.
My eyes trace
the perfect stripes
that lead to his eyes,
black jades
that contain me
in their frozen center.

When I blink,
the dream is not over,
but the tiger
is gone.

Golden Age

after the painting, *Woman Writing a Letter*, by Gerard ter Borch, 1655

The girl is writing a letter to her fiancé in the East Indies,
the tapestry on the half-naked table pulled back in haste.
She has a question about their engagement party –
the number of friends he plans to invite
to her parent's canal house on the Singel –
because what she wants cannot be put into words.
She had a dream and woke up in a sweat
thinking about him – or was it his friend Paul?
She wants to make sure he won't be at the party,
the way he stares at her with his probing blue eyes.

She holds the feather pen tightly
as she begins to daydream about her Derik
with one of the natives in the village.
Dark eyes lure him into a hut where the woman
has nothing but a straw mat, open fire, a pot –
the way she admires his uniform,
the brass buttons so shiny she can almost make out
her reflection before she opens each one.

Public Spaces

As I approach the security gate at the airport, I tell the guard I would prefer not to go into the X-ray machine. She yells out, *Male guard!* The man pulls me aside and tells me what he's going to touch with the front of his hands, what he's going to touch with the back. He wants to know if I want to do this in private. I say, *No, right here.* I hold out my arms and he begins to pat me down. Everyone watches as they stand in line, waiting to walk into the machine.

• • •

At the Met, I linger in front of Rembrandt's *Self-Portrait.* I'm drawn to his eyes, dark and tenacious. I try to imagine what they saw in 1660 from his window on the Rozengracht: the way the light illuminated peddlers on the street, selling cheese and herring from their wooden carts.

The hundreds of years his eyes have been watching from this canvas, and what they have seen: all the people gazing at him, thinking about the Golden Age, or his talent, or their own lives as they grow older – whether or not they still have the will to change.

Or perhaps they're thinking about nothing at all, and just stop because they should, because Rembrandt is, after all, Rembrandt.

• • •

In the 200-year-old Haman in central Turkey, men of all ages cluster in small groups. I imagine they're talking about Erdogan's repressive policies; their families, wives, girlfriends. As they walk around, they struggle to keep their tiny towels wrapped around their waists.

I lie on a marble slab as an old masseur scrubs my body. I'm more exposed than meets the eye – the dead layers, muscles so tense they only seem to harden as he presses into them. He begins to tell me a story and when he realizes I can't understand, he just smiles as he continues to scrub. He pours a tub of warm suds over me: a cleansing quilt.

• • •

I go to the theatre with Mother to see *Annie Get Your Gun*. I know it's the last time we'll go to the theatre together. Already in a wheelchair, her limbs are beginning to atrophy, her breathing becoming increasingly shallow. When Annie begins to sing, *I Can Do Anything Better Than You Can*, everyone laughs, and I begin to weep. Mother turns to me with an expression that says, *What's going on?* It's the first time I recall when we do not complete each other's thoughts.

The Corporation

The woman I had to lay off calls to whisper
I'm going to get you, and your family too.
I rush to the front desk to describe her –
red hair, small face, freckles.
The guard tells me to relax, he's sure it's only a threat

but I don't believe him.
I see the rage in her eyes when she spoke to me.
I see myself mouthing the lines I learned
from a script, words like *Opportunity*,
the big 'O' nothing but a gaping hole

both of us fall through together.
We tumble slowly,
wrestlers suspended in mid-air.
That's the part of the script the writers leave out:
the part where all the actors keep tumbling.

The Croissants

after the painting, *Jeanne Hébuterne, Seated,* by Amedeo
Modigliani, 1918

Perhaps Jeanne always knew her life would be short,
tied as it was to Amedeo's. She sits on their single bed,
the white cover reflecting the colors of Nice in winter,
raspberry, a touch of mauve and yellow –
the duvet and pillow puffed up, and Jeanne,
twenty and full with their first child.
Amedeo has a hunch it will be a girl
and he tells Jeanne how much he'll spoil her,
and then he goes on about the croissants
he'll buy every day from the bakery downstairs,
and then the toys, dresses, books, and of course
she'll be a painter so her room will be one big canvas.
He steps into the painting and kisses Jeanne on the forehead,
and she notices how hot he is, it must be the
fevers, and she embraces him, forces herself to imagine
how he'll walk through the door with the croissants
and they'll be so warm, the butter melts in his hands.

The Girl with the Pearl Earring

At the museum, the woman behind me remarks
how much the girl looks like Scarlett Johansson
and I begin to imagine that the book and movie
came first, a modern-day Vermeer so taken by Scarlett
that he decides to make the painting.

And how well he captures 17th century Delft!
I can see the girl rushing along the canal,
stopping at the market and calling out for *boerenkool,*
aardappelen, jonge kaas, volkorenbrood[11].
The young men try to engage her, but she knows

Vermeer is waiting. When she arrives at his studio,
she'll sit in her usual chair and turn her head towards him,
not a full turn, but just enough to relinquish part of her beauty,
the rest of her still the girl, somewhat obedient,
just beginning to flirt with words like, *nee* and *ja, misschien wel[12].*

Today is the last day of her sitting when he'll finish
the pearl earring and, in it, he'll capture
his world away from his wife and children, bills, parties –
only his colors: lapis lazuli, crimson, ochre, ecru –
in a drop of light, hanging gracefully from Scarlett's ear.

_____

[11.] kale, potatoes, young cheese, whole wheat bread
[12.] no and yes, perhaps

Pandemic

One day we will learn to live
with our solitude.
It will be borne of health,
not disease.
Your friends will call you
to find out what
made you happy today
and you can say:

I was taking a walk
through the neighborhood
and stopped when
I noticed
a hummingbird hovering
over a Bird-of-Paradise,
and for a moment
the earth fluttered.

When People are About to Die

When people are about to die, they like to
revisit their surroundings, to make sure,
perhaps, that nothing around them has changed,
neighbors still remember who they are.

A few days before Mother died, she asked me
to wheel her through the hall of the apartment building.
She could barely speak but she pointed and I understood.
We even knocked on a few doors and the neighbors

invited her in and asked her how she was doing.
She tried to talk about Father as though
he were still alive, that we would go back home
and he would be there, a warm meat loaf on the table.

During the pandemic, I often take strolls
through our neighborhood a few times a day.
I'm careful to take a different route each time,
to notice how much the world changes with each walk:

There, a blue jay alighting on our Liquid Amber,
a mother pushing her baby in a stroller
early one morning, pointing to the full moon
disappearing in the sky: *Look,* she says, *Look.*

Opening: After the Lockdown

My friends will have to forgive me as I rush back
to my tiny office under the house, familiar blue chair,

my background always a blur to the world
to hide the hot water heater and a bookcase

stacked with collections by my favorite poets:
Yeats, Stevens, Rilke, Amichai, Glück –

the people who help me navigate my life
even through the most expansive times.

Perhaps that is what the lockdown was meant
to teach me: how I can learn to keep my world

at bay, to appreciate even the people I know
from a distance – their blurred lives, faces covered,

voices muffled – so I have to listen even harder,
discover the pleasures of being vigilant.

Woman Takes a Selfie in Front of Klimt's *The Kiss*

The Belvedere, Vienna

The woman positions herself just
so, and then angles her cell phone
so she can appear to displace the *inamorada*.
Little does she care about interpretation,
the woman in the painting on her knees,
suggesting that she might not be equal to the man,
or perhaps Klimt is projecting himself
onto the woman and is begging
for a kind of love that can,
once and for all, end his isolation.
The woman's device is on a long stick
and she appears to be dancing with it.
Yes, they are partners waltzing
in this chandeliered room in the Belvedere,
the orchestra playing Strauss' *Blue Danube*,
and when she finds the perfect spot she stops,
slowly closes her eyes, and clicks a pic.

3

Remember that the light and the dark
are the same,
if you can,

if you can,
that the I
and the Thou are the same,

the above and the below,
the far and the near.
Embrace the words you cannot hear.

– Michael Palmer, from "Tbilisi Thoughts"

Memorial

Babyn Yar, March, 2022

The Russians strike Babyn Yar
as they try to "de-Nazify" Ukraine:
sounds of shattering glass,
the metallic smell of the afterlife.

A thick smoke fills the air –
here, where the Nazis murdered
over 30,000 Jews in two days.
As the Jews walked towards the ravine,
the Nazis ordered them to get undressed
and place their clothing into neat stacks:
dresses,
        pants,
                shirts,
                        underwear.

The black wisps of smoke weave together
like bodies joining a ceremonial dance –
and then they take on shapes so grotesque,
no one can describe what they are.

Coming to Prayer

It is not in the heavens.
– Deuteronomy 30:12

Finding faith is opening a window into the world:
a glimpse of the Himalayas, a curtain of waterfalls,
a flock of birds in the shape of an *aleph*.

• • •

First comes the Big Bang: the universe expands,
galaxies spread across the sky, the heavens
separate the waters above from the waters below.

• • •

The Zohar says nothing is known beyond the infinite
so it is called Beginning: a baby lamb, redwood sapling,
a dying woman counting her final breaths.

• • •

God puts Abraham to the test or is it
the other way around – our need for fear as great as
our need for angels, our need for words.

• • •

Preparing for ritual is ritual itself:
wrapping the *tallit* around one's shoulders –
shawl that envelops the generations.

• • •

The barrier protecting Gilo is dismantled:
a boy playing with a soccer ball
kicks it across an imaginary divide.

　　• • •

When we light the candles, we are complicit
with the dark: a family fleeing Kabul
hoping to find a safer life across a border.

　　• • •

In Deuteronomy, You shall love *Adonai* your God.
A man weeps, another man trembles:
It is not in the heavens.

In Other Words

We don't change the message.
The message changes us.
– Billboard at Zion Lutheran Church, Oakland

A word gets buried
so deeply in prayer,
I can only read the letters:
Yud, Hay, Vav, Hay.
They fly off the page –
a flock of skylarks
feathers the name for God.

In *The Zohar*, Rabbi Shim'on says:
When a word issued, it seemed to be one;
but as it was engraved in its place,
seventy branches appeared in that word…

I imagine those branches with faces –
my parents, grandparents, ancestors.
They have a secret for me:
When God no longer needs us,
we can all stop praying.

Exuberance

Holding back is passionate.
Robert Oppenheimer begins to imagine the atomic bomb.

Klinghoffer sits in a wheelchair on the *Aquille Lauro*.
Terrorists embark on a cruise ship, ramp to heaven.

My uncle never stops riding trains in WW II Europe.
The partisans are few, but they number in the millions.

The Proud Boys want to lead the way.
Civilizations disappear, sometimes without a trace.

The *Zohar* says the Blessed Holy One is hidden away.
A gate opens, a breath fills our lungs.

A Small Act of Kindness

after the painting, *Self-Portrait with Hat*, by Camille Pissarro,
1903

Regardless of his chronic eye infection,
Pissarro takes a dim view of the world:
With Dreyfus in jail, he's advised
to stay in his apartment on the Place Dauphine,
and that's where he paints,
watching Paris from his window –
across the street, the baker shutting his shop,
a woman in a fur coat walking her poodle.
He's sure that Dreyfus is innocent,
but there's little Pissarro can do as a Jew
except write letters to *L'Aurore*
claiming that Zola is right, a hero in fact,
leave it to artists to speak the truth.

Pissarro squints his eyes to focus on the baker
handing a brioche to a small boy. Surely,
this is what keeps me sane, he thinks,
to see a small act of kindness
and imagine it as a painting:
twilight at Pont Neuf,
the city about to be blanketed in snow
that will contain every color on his palette.

Jerusalem

In the Old City, a guide tells his group
it's safe to walk around, all the quarters
monitored by surveillance cameras.
I look up and see a steel gray lens
lilting back and forth,
an eye trying to anchor in time:
A man in a black hat and coat
crosses the road in front of a car
reading from his prayer book.
He mumbles in Hebrew
and then his voice begins to tremble –
a *yud* shimmers
like a butterfly stopped in mid-air.
Alongside him, a man in a *djellaba*
hears the muezzin's cries
and breaks into a run,
his urgent *Allahu ak-bar, Allahu ak-bar*
parting the crowd.

We go back to our apartment,
walls made of Jerusalem stone.
I stare at one piece until I see a face emerge:
a lion resting, merely resting.

Diaspora

I say *Kaddish* for my parents
at the Wailing Wall
and then find two stones
to take home
and place on their graves.

On the flight home,
the pilot announces
we'll stop on Cyprus to refuel:
the gas from Ben Gurion
might be contaminated with explosives.
I miss all my connections.

The journey of two stones
could have been so simple.

Tel Aviv Promenade

This afternoon
knows little about war –
the promenade full of
children riding tricycles,
jugglers surrounded
by young crowds,
parents smiling
behind their cameras.
Moshe says
we're only worried
about the borders,
this city is safe.

Nearby, a young clown
with one leg
blows up balloons.
A girl chooses
Mickey Mouse:
her quiet *Toda.*[13]

[13.] Thank you

Here I Am

On a business trip to Israel, I stay in a hotel
that used to be the largest movie theatre in Tel Aviv.
My room is lined with black and white photographs:
Dorothy Gish, Mary Pickford, Clark Gable.
In the lobby, the guests stand around and watch
clips of silent Laurel and Hardy movies.
They point to the screen, laughing periodically,
while they continue their small conversations –
a room full of birds making a cacophony of sounds:
Dutch, Chinese, German, French, English.

On the streets, the banter in Hebrew, signs
in the alphabet I studied for years in religious school
and still have no clue what the words mean.
I stop in front of a synagogue and try to read
a flyer by stringing sounds together.
It's *Shavuot*[14], so there's a drawing of Moses
with a long beard, standing next to a burning bush.
Moses stumbles over his words, but in the *Book of Exodus*
he's clear when he responds to God, *Hineni*[15],
the three syllables rising from his breath, quivering.

[14.] Shavuot is a Jewish holiday that – among other things – marks the revelation of the Torah to Moses and the Israelites at Mt. Sinai.
[15.] Here I am

Perspectives: Germany

At the airport bookstore in Frankfurt,
a recent edition of Anne Frank's diary on one shelf,
a new book about Hitler on the shelf below –
a British writer analyzing Hitler's appeal to the masses.
I can't see any of the other books in the bookcase –
just a row of photos of a smiling Anne Frank,
a row of photos of a scowling Adolph Hitler.

• • •

In Berlin, 2,711 gray concrete slabs –
a memorial to the murdered Jews of Europe.
But what about the other five-million,
nine-hundred ninety-seven thousand, two-hundred and
       eighty-nine?
The slabs would fill the city and countryside covered,
as they are, with a special coating to prevent graffiti,
made by the same company that produced Zyklon B.

• • •

1989: My parents are invited back to Germany.
Father is paraded down the main street of his hometown,
then welcomed into his house that was confiscated by the
parents and grandparents of the people in the parade.
The video camera is trained on Father as he walks
into his bedroom, points out the window to the small yard:
Früher haben wir hier gespielt,[16] he says, beaming.

[16.] We used to play here.

Defining the Light

after the painting, *Still Life*, by Pieter Claesz Soutman, 1647

Slices of pink herring –
small head resting on the edge
of the silver platter, eyes open –
terra cotta bowl brimming:
grapes, pomegranates, peaches.

I imagine a curl of lemon rind
dangling from the table,
my craving for metaphor
greater than my appetite
for raw fish.

Still Life with Cat and Fish

after the painting, *Still Life with Cat and Fish*, by Jean-Baptiste-Simeon Chardin, 1728

Nothing is still.
In a moment, the cat
will pounce on the dead fish
and start tearing it apart.
The scene will become a mess
of fish skin and bones,
the plate will fall to the ground
with a loud crash,
the room will smell of rotting sea life
and garlic –

but the painting will remain,
ticking.

Reading Spinoza at a Rest Stop on the I-5

I search for god in every corner
of the *Travel Center of America*:
between slices of turkey breast at Subway,
on lines leading to the restroom, in the impatient
sighs of a woman waiting to pay for a beef jerky.

After I unscrew the cap of my gas tank,
I imagine Spinoza at the adjacent pump –
a small man wearing his signature black cloak,
pumping gas into a first-generation silver Prius.
He tells me I'm trying too hard,
that god is thought itself, the very reason
I've embarked on my wonderful journey.

I screw the cap back on my tank, turn around
and he's gone, heading north on the I-5,
the *Travel Center* too electrified
to see even a single star in the sky.

The Window

after the painting, *The Window,* by Edouard Vuillard, 1894

The woman turns away from her bedroom window
as though the light might reveal something
she is not yet ready to know.
On the foot of the tightly-made bed,
a spray of roses and a book, waiting to be opened.
She always felt she had married too young
but her parents insisted on the engagement to her
fourth cousin – from such a good family,
with all of the men employed by the *Société Générale.*

In a few moments, the woman will move towards
the window to see if she recognizes anyone below.
Perhaps her friend Marie will be walking by
and she can call down to invite her to tea,
and they can spend the afternoon chatting
about the latest fashions from Paris, the woman's plans
for decorating her home in Provence.
But then she remembers how dreadfully boring
Marie becomes when she brings up the news.
No doubt, it would be the new Franco-Russian Alliance
her husband was chatting about this morning
when all she had wanted was to eat her croissant
in peace, the raspberry preserves dripping onto her plate.

Message: Sitka Sound

When I first spot them
I'm not sure what they are,
large torches, perhaps,
flames tapering into a soft glow.
And then, as if someone shouted,
they soar from the branches,
scores of eagles scouring the Sound.
An otter, attentive, flips over on its back
to protect its morning catch.

The water is balance as it holds
the early light framed by the shore –
red-throated loons walking beside
herons and egrets, flowers with names like
pearly everlasting, river beauty, harebell.
A dolphin pops up its nose near our kayak
and does it again and again,
right to left and left to right, tapping out
an urgency from another world.

Rescue

Khao Yai National Park, Thailand, 2019

From a distance,
they look like gray
boulders
tumbling down a waterfall:
a small elephant
followed by 12 larger ones.

The water is
fast,
forgiving.

When the baby
slipped,
the herd did not
stand a chance.

Dusk on the Rue St Lazare

after the painting, *Portrait of an Unknown Man Reading a Newspaper*, by Andre Derain, 1911-1914

The man wears a black suit and tie as he sits
on his red overstuffed chair reading *Le Journal*,
the paper folded neatly in half.
He's glum about the sudden turn in events:
The French begin to recapture Alsace
and Paris is jubilant, the bars serving
their vintage *Châteauneuf-du-Pape* –
but then the Germans launch their surprise,
the troops pouring in from Strasbourg,
an undertow of war.

Behind the man, a blue curtain is tied back.
In a moment he'll get up,
go to the kitchen and pour himself a Pernod.
As the anise rises from the warm elixir,
embellishing his thoughts,
he walks behind his chair and, with a deep sigh,
yanks off the tie holding back the curtain,
the big blue canvas flooding the room.

Caesura

after the painting, *Tea*, by Henri Matisse, 1919

The Treaty of Versailles just signed, the two women
sit under a chestnut tree in Issy-les-Moulineaux.
Marguerite talks about the repair work
that needs to be done on the house –
a new roof, fresh coat of paint in every room –
and how difficult it will be to find the best tradesmen,
now that all the soldiers are back looking for work.
Henriette is thrilled about the sets Matisse
is designing for Diaghilev's ballet even though
there's no doubt they'll steal the show from the dancers.
Her shoe dangles from her right foot as she pauses

to look at the dog, the only creature in the painting
staring at Matisse, who no doubt has a pocketful of treats,
perhaps some chocolate for the ladies.
Marguerite will soon reach across the table
for her tea and tell Henriette she must stay for dinner:
She and Matisse plan to open a bottle of Bordeaux
they've been saving until the war ends.
In fact, they'll celebrate the end of all wars
as they sit in the dining room next to a fire,
enjoy their meal of steak, fried potatoes, a green salad –
not a moment too soon to recount their blessings.

Meditation

When the sun comes up,
our yellow lab jumps on the bed,
lays the length of her body
alongside mine,
and rests her cheek on my cheek.
She could lie like this for hours,
oblivious to everything
but her own comfort,
and I try to appease her
by trying impossibly
to slow my breath to hers,
grateful to be woken
into this stillness.

Doga

Mornings, my dog and I
do yoga together in the bathroom:
She does her Downward Dog
and I, the Humble Warrior
as I begin to approach my day –
the long commute, meetings
about the latest changes in our software and,
after work, a board meeting at the non-profit,
followed by a business call to India.
Roxie sits patiently as I brush my teeth
and prepare to go to the pool
in the dark, cold morning,
reluctant to face the 2000 yards.

When I look down, she's staring at me,
her face now at an angle, poised:
a question mark.

Distant Voices

Doctors say you can control the images in your dreams.
Mother and Father, holding hands, enter the apartment.

In Japan, scientists try putting lithium into the water supply.
No cavities, the world smiles.

A Wall St. CEO says investment bankers are doing God's work.
Moses dies before he reaches the Promised Land.

In Accra, children tear apart computers they receive for the copper
    and brass.
When minds are starving, the belly is the last to go.

In the London tabloid, *The War in Afghanistan is a Bust.*
The sound of gunfire in Yemen drowns out the muezzin.

Phone Banking for Biden

A few days before the election
and a 74-year-old woman in Ohio
is still undecided. I begin by asking her
if she enjoys receiving Medicare
and then anticipate the other questions I'd like to ask –
whether or not she has a granddaughter
who might want to make decisions about her body,
or a grandson serving in the military.
I'll ask her if she knows how our economic crisis started
and the number of blue-collar jobs
that have already been created this month.

The woman tells me she's tired of receiving calls,
Can't the world just leave me alone,
and I imagine hanging up and her phone ringing
continuously. There's nothing she can do
to stop the ringing in her home, in her head.
Even after she turns off her phone service
and decides never to read a newspaper
or watch the news on TV,
the birds will begin to sound like ring tones
and she'll want to answer them.
She imagines she'll know what to say.

The Invisible

after the painting, *Cape Cod Morning,* by Edward Hopper, 1950

It doesn't really matter what she's looking at,
be it a rabbit or a fox running across the field.
The truth is, the creature has now become a thought:
her husband, gone for over an hour
when he said he would only be running into town
to pick up a newspaper and a jar of honey.
She was having a hard time sleeping
and the only antidote to her insomnia
(or so she thought) was a cup of warm milk,
and merely watching the honey drip into it,
the thick gold strand being absorbed
by the warm, white liquid, was enough
to calm her, to even allow her to enjoy
being alone in the kitchen at 2AM.

She barely hears the green Buick as her husband
drives it up the path, the sound of the gravel
as familiar to her as the ticking of the kitchen clock.
He tells her he was delayed because he ran into Bill –
his son just shot in Korea, and he and his wife
awaiting word about his condition. She snaps to,
mumbles something about the state of the world,
all the talk about a nuclear bomb and she wonders
if they'll ever be safe, even here on Cape Cod
where tonight she can only imagine the waves
crashing over each other again and again,
the moon disappearing into each fold.

Ushering at the San Francisco Opera

From the end of the long line of patrons
waiting for me to escort them to their seats –
the Carmen wannabe in the floor-length red chiffon gown,
black hair pulled back, fashioned into a bun,
the man in a tux walking and reading his program
through rose glasses perched on the tip of his nose –
my friend Bill shouts to me: *Hey Stewart,*
didn't I see you naked at the pool this morning?

Everyone chuckles as I look down to make sure I'm clothed.
And then I recall the 200-yard medley we did
in our Masters group at 6:00 that morning, my legs
still tight because I didn't stretch enough after the swim.
Carmen tells me she's a swimmer as well
and just completed the two-mile race from Alcatraz.
In fact, everyone shares their exercise routines with me
as I escort them to their seats –
the woman preparing for her first triathlon,
the man trying his hand at boxing,
the woman who does Bikram Yoga every morning.

The lights dim and my patrons appear restless in their seats.
When Irene Roberts begins her first aria,
the triathlete stretches her arms across her shoulders,
imagines the light shimmering on the pool and dives in,
one arm stretching out then pulling the water
hard along the length of her long body.
She's swimming just above the surface now
as she listens to Carmen sing sweetly about love,
the rebellious bird that no one can tame.

About the Author

Stewart Florsheim was born in New York City, the son of a Holocaust survivor and a refugee from Hitler's Germany. He has received several awards for his poetry and has been widely published in magazines and anthologies.

Stewart was the editor of *Ghosts of the Holocaust*, an anthology of poetry by children of Holocaust survivors (Wayne State University Press, 1989). He wrote the poetry chapbook, *The Girl Eating Oysters* (2River, 2004). In 2005, Stewart won the Blue Light Book Award for *The Short Fall from Grace* (Blue Light Press, 2006). His collection, *A Split Second of Light*, was published by Blue Light Press in 2011 and received an Honorable Mention in the San Francisco Book Festival, honoring the best books published in the Spring of 2011. Stewart's new collection, *Amusing the Angels*, won the Blue Light Book Award in 2022.

Stewart has been awarded residencies from Artcroft and the Kimmel Harding Nelson Center for the Arts. He has held readings throughout the Bay Area, as well as in New York, Boston, London, and Jerusalem. He also writes non-fiction and is a contributor to KQED's *Perspective* series. Stewart sits on the board of directors of two non-profits – Jewish Family and Community Services of the East Bay and End of Life Choices California. He lives in the Bay Area with his wife.

Also by Stewart Florsheim

CPSIA information can be obtained
at www.ICGtesting.com
Printed in the USA
BVHW042339060223
658028BV00004B/94